Savvy

Crafty Creations

# Seamless Sewing Projects

by Veronica Yang

CAPSTONE PRESS
a capstone imprint

Savvy Books are published by Capstone Press,
1710 Roe Crest Drive, North Mankato, Minnesota 56003
www.mycapstone.com

**Library of Congress Cataloging-in-Publication Data**
Library of Congress Cataloging-in-Publication Data is available on the Library
of Congress website.

ISBN: 978-1-5157-7445-7 (library binding)
ISBN 978-1-5157-7449-5 (eBook PDF)

**Editorial Credits**
Marissa Bolte, editor; Juliette Peters, designer; Sarah Schuette, photo stylist;
Marcy Morin, scheduler; Kathy McColley, production specialist

**Photo Credits**
All images by Capstone Studio/Karon Dubke except Shutterstock: Roberto Sorin,
31 (right), grafvision, 31 (inset), ADragan, 33 (bottom); Veronica Yang, 22, 25 (top
left, bottom left, bottom middle), 33 (middle left, middle right), 39 (middle left),
45 (bottom right)

*Note from the author:* Sewing is not a common hobby for
teenagers. Making a book about sewing as a teenager is
even stranger. For me sewing was a second nature due to
my mother's career and hobby. I was lucky to have a creative
and inspirational mother who motivated me to create and
design. I want show younger audiences to be also inspired
and achieve their goals in their life. -Veronica Yang

Printed and bound in the USA.
010845S18

# Table of Contents

# Sewing is Sweet

Sewing is sweet! Fabric comes in thousands of colors and patterns, and can be purchased at any craft or sewing store. Do you see a fashion you can't live without? Try DIY-ing it! From pillows to blankets to bags and baskets, fabric can do it all. And you can, too!

All the projects in this book use cotton fabric. Work your way up from fat quarters and you'll be unraveling rolls of fancy fabric in no time!

# Fabric is Fun!

Fabric comes in thousands of colors and patterns. You can get it by the yard (36 inches) at craft and fabric stores. Bolts are typically between 45 and 60 inches wide. Most cotton fabrics are 44 inches wide. To put that into perspective, a yard of cotton fabric measures 36-by-44 inches.

There are many different sizes of specially precut fabric, from fat quarters to layer cakes to jelly rolls. Many projects in this book use fat quarters, which measure 18-by-22 inches.

# Basic Info

Start simple! There are some basic tips and techniques that can help you in your sewing journey.

## Backstitching

Sew a few stitches back and forth to secure loose ends. Normally backstitching is always used unless it is specified not to.

## Topstitching

Stitching on the right side of the fabric for decorative use.

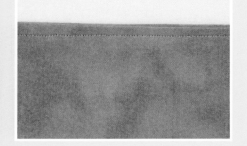

## Basting stitch

Use long hand or machine stitches to temporarily hold two or more pieces together.

## Slipstitch

Thread a needle and tie a knot at the end. Poke the needle into the fold of the fabric and pull the thread taut to the knot between the layers of fabric. Insert the needle into the fold of opposite layer of fabric, and pull the thread taut. Repeat until the required area is closed. Tie a knot to secure it, and cut off excess thread.

The slipstitch is used to keep an opening secure without any stitches visible.

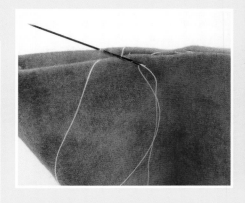

## Right Side/Wrong Side

The right side of the fabric is the side with the pattern. The wrong side is the faded side.

Measurements are important when you're sewing! Keep this chart handy for easy metric conversions.

| US | METRIC |
|---|---|
| $\frac{1}{8}$ inch | .125 cm |
| $\frac{1}{4}$ inch | .64 cm |
| $\frac{1}{2}$ inch | 1.3 cm |
| 1 inch | 2.5 cm |
| 9 inches | $\frac{1}{4}$ yard |
| 1 foot | 30.5 cm |
| 18 inches | $\frac{1}{2}$ yard |
| 27 inches | $\frac{3}{4}$ yard |
| 3 feet | 1 yard |

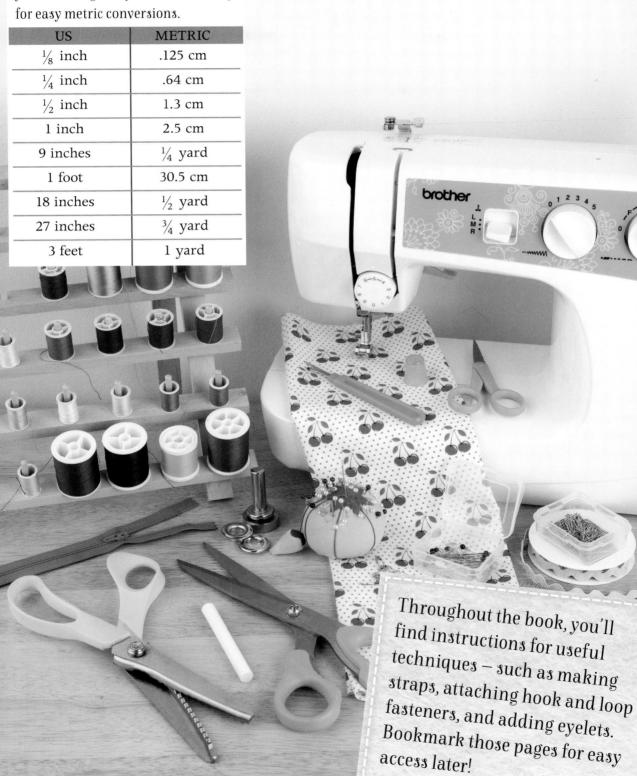

Throughout the book, you'll find instructions for useful techniques – such as making straps, attaching hook and loop fasteners, and adding eyelets. Bookmark those pages for easy access later!

# Quilt Cushion Cover

## Materials

· four square pieces of 10 ¾-inch fabric for front

· two pieces of 20 ¾-by-16-inch fabric for back

· 20-inch square cushion

· four tassels (optional)

Brighten your space with a colorful pillowcase! Pick fun fabrics that coordinate with your furniture, or go crazy and choose the loudest patterns you can find.

**1** Place one quilt piece on top of the other piece with its right sides together. Pin one edge, and sew them together, leaving a 3/8 inch seam allowance. Repeat with the other two squares. Open the rectangles.

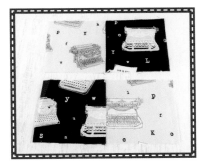

**2** Stack the rectangles on top of each other, right sides together. Pin one long edge. Then sew the rectangles together to make the front of the pillowcase. Set aside.

**3** Set one back piece on your workstation. Fold the longer edge of the piece down ½-inch. Then fold again. Use an iron for crisp folds. Then sew along the edge to keep the fold in place.

**4** Repeat step 3 with the second back piece.

**5** Line up three edges of a back piece with the front piece. The right sides should be together. The folded edge of the back piece should face in. Pin and sew the three edges.

**6** Repeat step 5 with the second back piece. This piece should line up with the opposite edge of the front piece.

**7** Trim the corner seam. Flip the pillowcase inside out. Then add a pillow!

## To Add Tassels:

**1** After step 2, pin the tassels in place on the wrong side of the pillow front. There should be one in each corner, and the tassels should face in.

**2** Baste the tassels in place. Continue with the remaining steps.

**Tip:**

If you don't have tassels, you can use embroidery floss. Just bunch the floss together, tie an end, and trim the loops.

9

# Fat Quarter Quilt Blanket

You'll never be cold again after you've made your first quilt blanket! With a few fat quarters and some fuzzy fleece, you'll be covered no matter how chilly it is.

## Materials

- six fat quarters
- 1 ½ yard of 44-inch-wide fleece or minky fabric

**1** Arrange the fat quarters the way you want them on your blanket.

**2** Stack two fat quarters together, right sides in. Pin and sew one shorter side.

**3** Repeat step 2 with the remaining pairs. Unfold all the fat quarters. You should have three rectangles.

**4** Match two rectangles together, right sides in. Pin and sew the longer end.

**5** Repeat step 4 to attach the third rectangle.

**6** Place the fleece fabric onto your workspace, with the right side up. Lay it as flat as you can.

**7** Set the fat quarters on top of the fleece, right side down. Smooth out any wrinkles.

**8** Pin all four edges together. Cut off any excess fleece.

**9** Sew around the edges, leaving a 5-inch opening on the bottom.

### Tip:

To make a smaller lap blanket, use 4 fat quarters instead of 6. You'll only need 1 yard of fleece.

**Continued on the next page...**

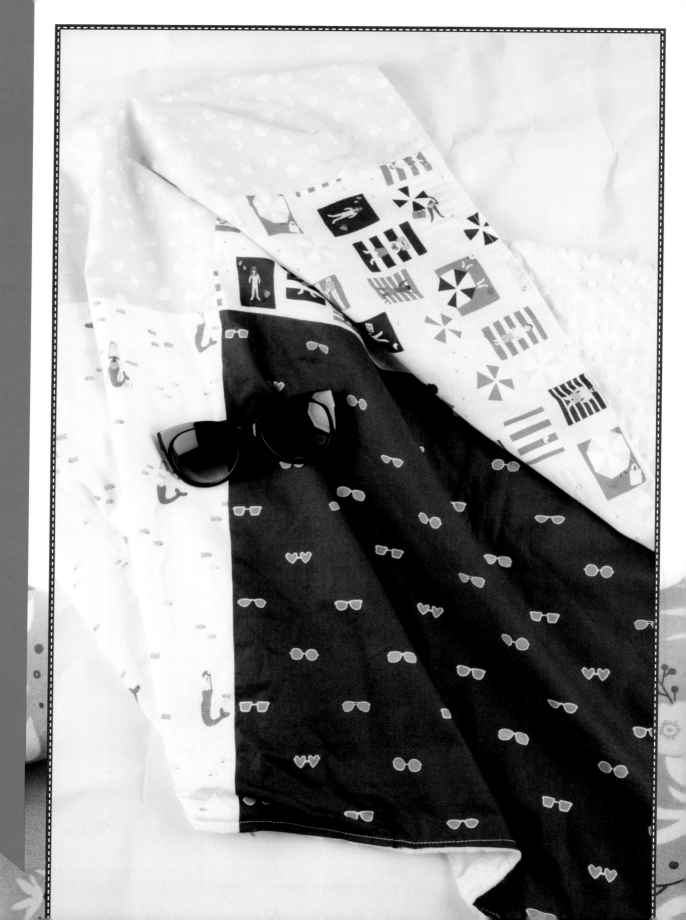

**10** Trim the corners. Then flip the blanket right side out, making sure everything is even.

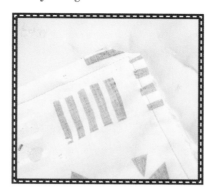

**11** Pin and topstitch the opening.

**12** Topstitch along the remaining edges of the blanket.

## Note:

Trim the excess fabric at the corners before turning projects right side out. This helps the finished corners look neater.

# Headband

Not sure what to do with a spare square of fabric? Turn it into something you'll see — and use — every day.

## Materials

· 1 fat quarter of fabric
· 1 ¼-inch-wide elastic band for garments

## Cut

· four pieces of 2 ½-by-22-inch fabric

### Tip:

Scissors are one of the most important tool any sewer has. Buy fabric scissors — and keep them separate from scissors used for paper! Using them on paper will dull them.

Pinking scissors are usually only used for decoration purposes, preventing the seams from fraying or to simply clip curved corners.

1 Place two fabric strips on top of each other, right sides together. Stitch the long edges together.

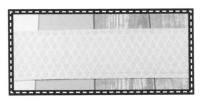

2 Turn the fabric tube right-side-out.

3 Repeat steps 1 and 2 with the other fabric strips.

4 Fold all the short ends of the fabric in 3/8-inch.

5 Cut the elastic band. Make it 3 inches for a loose fit, or 2 inches for a snug fit.

6 Loop the fabric strips around each other, and match both ends.

7 Tuck the ends of the elastic into the fabric tubes.

8 Pin and topstitch the ends of the tubes to the elastic.

# Pet Bed

Your four-legged friends are family too, so why not let them sit around in style? This pet bed is both cute and comfortable.

## Materials

· 1 yard of fabric for the top
· 1 yard of fabric for the bottom
· fiber filling

## Cut

· one 30-inch square piece of fabric for the top
· one 30-inch square piece of fabric for the bottom

**1** Lay the top piece of fabric flat on your work surface. Measure and cut out out 3-inch squares at each corner.

**2** Repeat step 1 with the bottom piece.

**3** Set the top and bottom pieces on top of each other, with the right sides together. Pin and sew all the outside, leaving the square corners unsewn. Leave a 5-inch opening along one edge too.

**4** Starting at one corner, match the sewn edges of the fabric together. Pin and stitch together.

**5** Repeat step 4 with the remaining corners.

**6** Use the 5-inch opening to flip the fabric right side out. Stuff the pillow with fiber filling.

**7** Pin and sew the opening shut.

# Felt Cupcakes

Cool colors and fun prints can help you express yourself when you're out and about. Give your sewing stuff an upgrade too! Replace the tiny tomatoes and simple strawberries in your sewing bag with cute cupcakes.

## Materials

- 9-by-12-inch felt sheet for the cupcake
- 9-by-12-inch felt sheet for the icing
- 9-by-12-inch felt sheet for the cupcake toppers
- fiber fill
- seed beads or pearls
- fabric glue

## Cut

- 6-inch circle for the cupcake (a)
- 2-inch circle for the cupcake bottom (b)
- 4-inch circle for the frosting (c)
- 1-inch circle for the frosting bottom (d)
- 2, 1.5, 1, and 0.5-inch circles for the cupcake toppers (e–h)

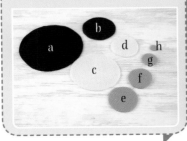

**1** Sew a running stich all around the edge of the cupcake piece. When you reach the end, do not cut the thread. Pull the thread to make a ball.

**2** Stuff the cupcake with fiber fill.

**3** Tie a knot on the string and cut.

**4** Place the cupcake bottom over the opening of the cupcake. Sew around the edges until it securely covers the opening.

**5** Sew a running stitch around the edge of the 4-inch frosting circle. Do not tie or cut the stitch. Pull the string until it looks like a small cushion.

**6** Stuff with fiber fill. Tie a knot to secure the frosting.

**7** Place the 1-inch frosting bottom piece on the opening of the frosting. Sew it around until it securely covers the opening.

**8** Stack the cupcake topper pieces on top of each other. Sew the pieces together.

**9** Sew the beads or pearls to the topper.

**10** Use fabric glue to attach the frosting to the cupcake.

**11** Glue the topper to the cupcake.

19

# Wrap Skirt

This simple skirt will teach you several more sewing skills – how to make straps, how to make gathers, how to do bias binding, and how to attach a hook and loop fastener. Once you've mastered these, you'll have a wrap skirt for every day of the week!

## Materials

- 2 ½ yards of fabric
- 6-inch hook and loop fastener

## Cut

- one 2-by-38-inch piece of fabric, for bias binding
- two 2-by-22 ½-inch pieces of fabric, for straps
- one 64 ½-by-26-inch piece of fabric, for skirt

### Tip:

Throughout the book the word "press" will appear often. This is a sewing term that means "iron".

Because the projects in this book are made with cotton, use the heat setting for cotton. Adjust the settings for other types of fabric.

**1** Follow steps 1–4 of the Making Bias Binding and Straps instructions on page 22 for the bias binding. Do not sew. Set aside.

**2** Follow steps 1–5 of the Making Bias Binding and Straps instructions for the straps. Set aside.

**3** Lay the skirt fabric on your workspace. Double fold the bottom edge up ½-inch. Press and pin into place.

**4** Repeat on the sides of the skirt. Stitch along the folded edges.

**5** Gather the skirt piece along the top edge. Follow the instructions on making gathers on page 22.

**6** Match the skirt gather with the bias binding.

**7** Follow the Attaching Bias Binding steps on page 23, and cover the gathers completely.

**8** Pin one of the strap pieces to the end of the skirt, and stitch into place.

**9** Wrap the skirt around your waist until it fits perfectly to your size. Mark where the end of the skirt touches. Pin and sew the second strap at the mark.

**10** Follow the instructions on page 23 for Attaching Hooks and Loops to add fasteners to the ends of the skirt.

# Making Bias Binding and Straps

**1** Fold ½-inch of fabric in on the short ends. The wrong sides of the fabric should touch.

**2** Fold the fabric in half the long way, with the wrong sides together. Press firmly to create a crease.

**3** Open the fabric and set on your workstation, with the wrong side up. Fold the bottom of the fabric in, lining the edge up with the center crease. Repeat with the top of the fabric.

**4** If you are making bias binding, stop here.

**5** To make a strap, fold the fabric in half, with the edges on the inside. Topstitch 1/8 inch around all the edges.

# Making Gathers

Lengthen your stitches to a basting stitch (the longest stitch on your sewing machine). Sew two lines of basting stitches. Do not backstitch the ends. Pull the threads at one end until the fabric has bunched to your liking.

# How to Attach Bias Binding

**1** Pin the raw edges of the binding in place. The right sides should touch. Stitch along the crease line.

**2** Fold the binding over the raw edge.

**3** Pin and sew the binding into place.

## Attaching Hooks and Loops

**1** Cut out the hook and loop tape to the size you need.

**2** Separate the hook side from the loop side. Place one side on the fabric.

**3** Pin and sew all four edges of the side, backstitching at both ends.

**4** Place the other side to the corresponding side of the fabric. Repeat step 3.

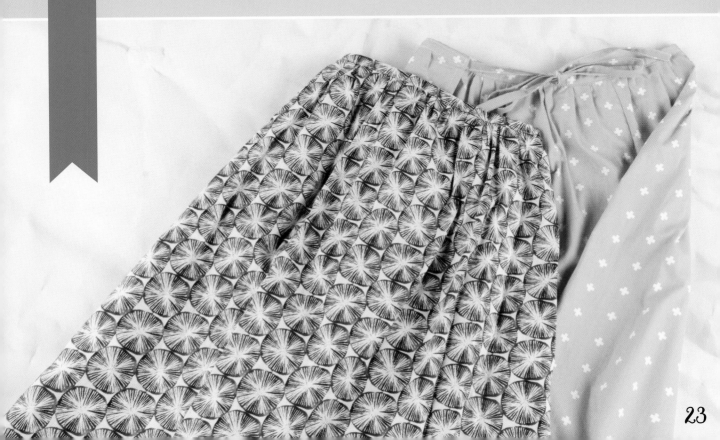

# Little Big Clutch Bag

Lead the accessory game by bringing bags that burst with color and style. Make one for every outfit!

## Materials

· 1 yard of fabric for the exterior

· 1 yard of fabric for lining

· 1 set of sew-on snaps

· 1/4 yard of 3/8 inch ribbon or fabric strap

· chain handle

## Cut

· one 10-by-29 ¾-inch piece of fabric for exterior

· one 10-by-29 ¾-inch interior

· two 1 1/2-inch pieces of ribbon or fabric strap

HANDMADE

### Tip:

Make each project your own by adding a tag or label! These small accents show your projects were made with love. Check Etsy for a wide variety.

**1** Follow the instructions to curve the corners on one end of the exterior and lining fabric pieces. The curved corners will be the flap.

**2** Set the exterior fabric on your work surface, wrong side up. Measure and mark 6 1/4 inches from the top edge.

**3** Set a piece of ribbon or strap on the mark. Fold the ribbon in half, and baste into place. Repeat on the opposite side of the fabric.

**4** Stack the exterior piece and the lining piece, with the right sides touching. Sew them together, leaving a 4-inch opening at the bottom.

**5** Follow the instructions to clip the corners.

**6** Flip the bag right side out. Press the bag so it is even and flat. Close the opening by topstitching around the bag.

**7** Measure and mark 5 ¾ inches from the bottom of the bag. Repeat three more times.

5 ¾"    5 ¾"    5 ¾"    5 ¾"

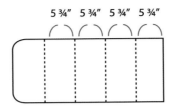

**8** Starting at the bottom of the fabric, make accordion folds along your marked lines. Leave the rounded flap unfolded. Pin and sew the sides.

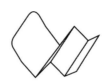

**9** Mark where you want the snaps. Then sew them on.

**10** Attach the chain strap to the ribbon loops.

## Curving the Corners

Curve the edges by using circular items such as cups or rolls of tape. Place the circular item on the corner and trace it with fabric chalk. Cut through the traced line.

## Clipping and Trimming the Seam

Cut small "v" shapes along the curved edge. This keeps the fabric from bunching on the inside.

# DIY Tote Bag

Carry everything you need – including your sewing supplies! – in this quick DIY tote bag.

## Materials

· 1 yard of fabric for the exterior
· 1 ½ yards of webbing
· 1 yard of fabric for lining

## Cut

· one 14-by-32 ¾-inch fabric for the exterior
· one 14-by-32 ¾-inch fabric for the lining
· two pieces of webbing, 18 3/8-inches long

**1** Fold the exterior piece in half horizontally, with the wrong sides touching. Make a mark along the entire crease with chalk. Unfold the fabric.

**2** At one end of the fabric, measure and mark 4 inches from the center line. Repeat on the other side.

**3** Place both ends of the webbing over the 4-inch marks. Make sure the webbing isn't twisted. Then baste it to the fabric.

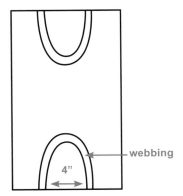

webbing

4"

**4** Repeat steps 2 and 3 on the other end of the fabric.

**5** Stack the lining piece onto the exterior fabric, with the right sides together. Sew around the edges, leaving a 4-inch opening on one side. Trim the corner seam.

**6** Flip the bag right side out, and topstitch around the bag.

**7** Fold the bag in half. The handles should touch and the inside should face out. Pin and sew 1/8-inch from both edges.

**8** Turn the bag so the exterior faces out, and press.

# Wall Storage

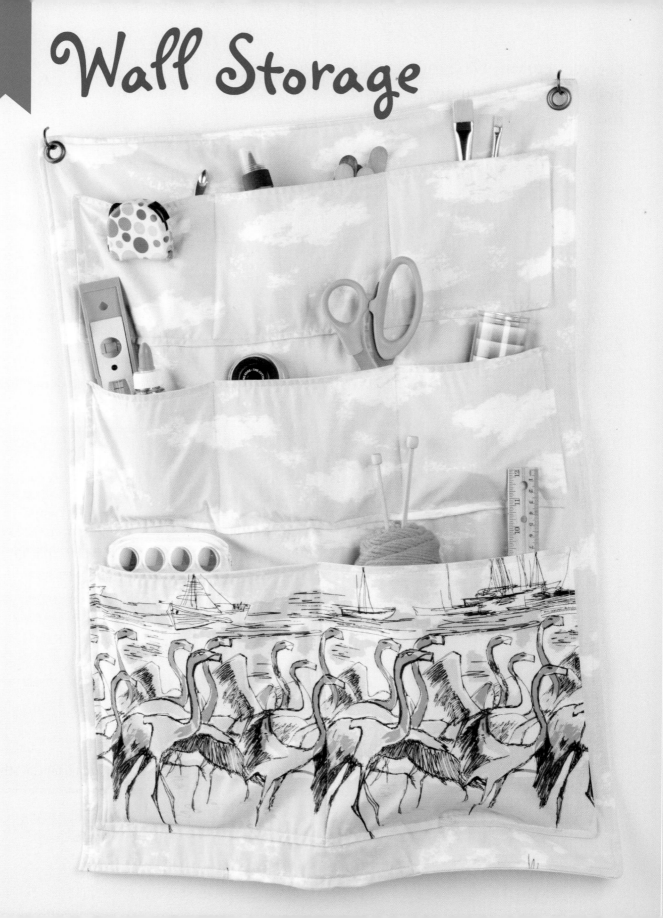

Keep your essentials close with this pocket-filled wall storage project. Hang it in a handy place, or carry it with you from room to room.

## Materials

- 1 ½ yards of fabric for the body
- 1 yard of fabric for the small pockets
- 1/3 yard of fabric for the large pocket
- 2 pairs of 3/8-inch eyelets and eyelet setter

## Cut

- one 21 ½-by-29 ¼-inch piece of fabric for the front of the body
- one 21 ½-by-29 ¼-inch piece of fabric for the back of the body
- four 19 ¾-by-6 ¾-inch pieces of fabric for the small pockets
- two 19 ¾-by-10 ¾-inch pieces for the big pocket

**1** Place the front and back pieces together, right sides touching. Pin and sew 3/8 inch from the edges, leaving a 5-inch opening along the bottom.

**2** Repeat step 1 with the pocket fabrics to make two small pocket pieces and one large pocket piece.

**3** Trim the corners of all the pieces, and turn right side out.

**4** Topstitch around the outside of the largest piece. Topstitch just the top edges of the pocket pieces.

**5** Set the large pocket piece onto the body piece. Center it, leaving 1 ½ inch of the body showing on the bottom. Pin the pocket in place.

**6** Measure and mark 1 ½ inches from the top of the large pocket. Line up one of the small pockets with the mark, and pin in place.

**7** Repeat step 6 for the other small pocket.

**Continued on the next page...**

29

**8** Make marks 1/3 and 2/3 across the small pockets. Sew around the sides and bottom of each small pocket. Then sew along the marks you just made.

**9** Make a mark in the center of the large pocket. Sew around the sides and bottom of the pocket. Then sew up the centerline mark.

**10** Have an adult help you install eyelets in the top corners of the body piece.

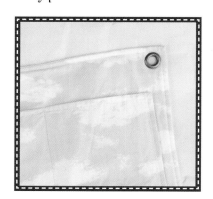

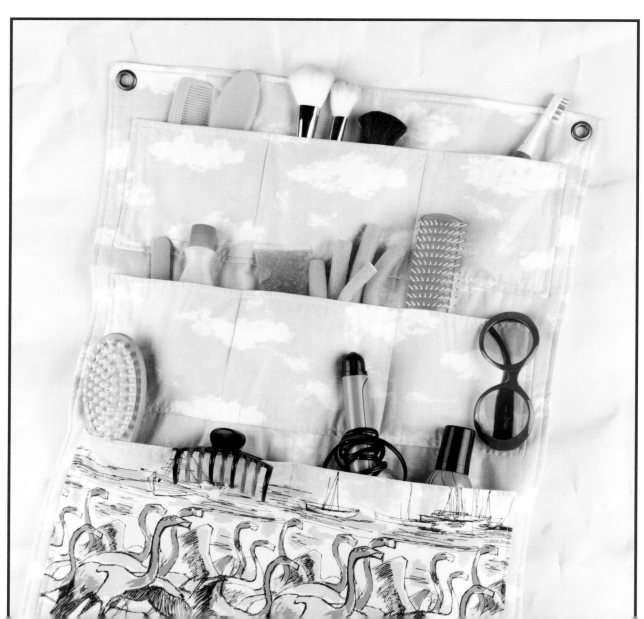

# Installing Eyelets

**1** Trace the inside eyelet on to the desired area with chalk or a washable fabric pen. Punch or cut out the hole.

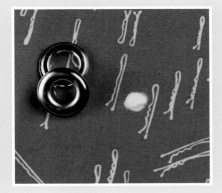

**2** Place an eyelet on the anvil with the barrel pointing up.

**3** Place the fabric hole over the eyelet. The wrong side of the fabric should face up.

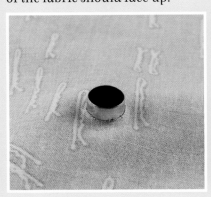

**4** Put the eyelet washer on top of the barrel. Its teeth should face down.

**5** Place the setter tool through the eyelet hole. Gently hammer the eyelet until it is securely fixed to the fabric.

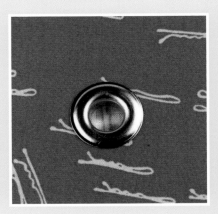

**Tip:**

Erasable fabric pens are best for precise marking and tracing, but you can also use chalk.

Chalks come in various types such as pencils, mechanicals, and in chalk wheels. Some chalks are hard to use for detailed marking. However, it is fine for simple tracing.

**Tip:**

Eyelet setters have many different types and sizes. They are used to punch holes on materials for installing eyelets.

# Zipper Pencil Case

Make your art supplies stand out with a pencil case created by you! You'll never get your case confused with someone else's again.

## Materials

· 1 fat quarter of fabric for exterior

· 1 fat quarter of fabric for lining

· all-purpose zipper

## Cut

· two 9 ½-by-5 ½-inch fabric piece for exterior

· two 9 ½-by-5 ½-inch fabric piece for lining

· one 9- or 10-inch zipper

1 Place an exterior and lining piece right-sides-together. Pin and sew around the fabric, leaving a 3-inch opening on one side. Trim the corner.

2 Flip the fabric right-side-out. Press flat.

3 Repeat step 2 with the other exterior and lining pieces.

4 Line one side of the zipper, right side up, with a long edge of the exterior fabric. Pin and sew into place.

5 Repeat step 4 with the other side of the zipper. Topstitch along the exterior, close to the zipper coil. Make sure the seams are facing the lining side, not the zipper.

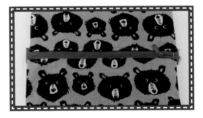

6 Fold the pencil case in half with the exterior sides together. Pin and sew around the pencil case.

7 Flip the bag exterior-side-out, and press.

## Tip:

A 10-inch zipper will give you plenty to work with! But a 9-inch zipper will work OK too.

# Fabric Bin

The words "storage bin" conjure up boring boxes and plastic containers. But you can whip up your own stylish bins with a few quick stitches.

## Materials

· ½ yard of fusible interfacing
· ½ yard of fabric for lining
· ½ yard of fabric for exterior

## Cut

· two pieces of of 14-by-14 ½-inch fusible interfacing
· two pieces of of 14 ¾-by-15 ¼-inch fabric for lining
· two pieces of of 14 ¾-by-15 ¼-inch fabric for exterior

1 Follow package instructions to attach the fusible interfacing to the wrong side of the lining.

2 Draw a 7-inch square on the bottom two corners of both the exterior and lining pieces. Cut the corners out.

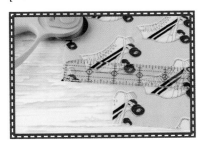

3 Place the two exterior pieces together. The right sides should touch.

4 Sew around the fabric, leaving the top edge and corner squares unstitched. Repeat with the lining.

5 Flip the fabric onto its side, with the seams facing up. Pinch a bottom corner and match the seams together. Pin and stitch into place.

6 Repeat step 5 with the lining.

7 Flip the lining right-side-out. Set it inside the exterior piece, right sides together. Sew around the top, leaving a 3-inch opening.

8 Flip the bin right-side-out, and press.

9 Topstitch along the top edge. Fold the edge down, to show off both the interior and exterior fabrics.

# Ruffle Half Apron

This ruffled apron will refresh your memory on sewing straps and bias binding. The hardest part will be deciding what you want to bake in your apron afterward!

## Materials

· 1 yard of fabric

## Cut

· one 44-by-3 ½-inch fabric for strap

· one piece of 34-by-17 ½-inch fabric for apron

**1** Follow the instructions on page 21 to make a strap, but fold in all the edges 3/8 inch instead of ½ inch.

**2** Double fold the side and bottom edges of the apron in ½-inch. Press and sew, leaving the top seam raw.

**3** Gather the raw edge of the apron until it is 21 ½-inches across.

**4** Mark 8 inches from one end of the strap.

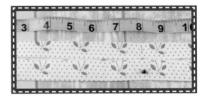

**5** Line a top corner of the apron up with the mark you just made on the strap. Then follow the instructions for adding bias binding on page 22.

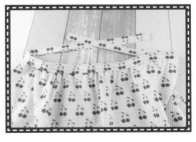

Sew the strap along the apron's top edge.

# Rollup Pencil Case

Everyone has a favorite pen, pencil, or other writing utensil. Keep yours from getting lost in the shuffle with a rolled pencil case.

## Materials

- 1 fat quarter of fusible interfacing
- 1 fat quarter for exterior
- 1 fat quarter for lining
- suede lace
- 1-inch button

## Cut

- 1 12-inch square piece of interfacing
- one 12 ½-inch square piece for exterior
- one 12 ½-inch square piece for lining
- three to four 17 1/2-inch length of suede lace

**1** Lay the exterior piece flat on your workstation. Press the fusible interfacing onto the wrong side of the lining. Measure and mark 3 ¾ inches from any side of the top corner.

**2** Place the suede laces on the marked area. Baste them in place.

**3** Place the exterior and lining piece together, with the right sides touching.

**4** Pin and sew around the edges of the fabric, leaving a 3-inch opening on one side.

**5** Trim the corners. Flip the pencil case right side out and press.

**6** Fold the bottom of the case up 4 ¼ inch. Pin and topstitch to make a pocket.

**7** Make marks 3 7/8 inches and 7 ¾ inches across. Sew up to divide the large pocket into three smaller pockets.

**8** Attach the button to exterior fabric, directly over the suede straps. To use, roll up the pencil case and wrap the suede laces around the sides. Loop the laces around the button to keep the case closed.

# Bookmark

Mark your place with a splash of color that pops off the page. Sew one up for every genre and keep your reading list color-coded.

## Materials

· two scrap pieces of fabric
· suede cording
· beads

## Cut

· one piece of 3 ¾-by-8 ¾-inch fabric for top
· one piece of 3 ¾-by-2-inch fabric for bottom
· two 6 ½ inch pieces of suede cording
· one piece of 3 ¾-by-10-inch fabric for back

**1** Line the bottom piece up with the short end of the top piece. The right sides should touch. Pin and sew together.

**2** Press the seam down.

**3** Center the suede cording in the middle of the bookmark. They should be on the opposite end of the bottom piece. Baste the cords into place.

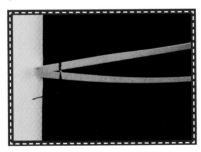

**4** Line up the back and front pieces with the right sides together. Sew around the bookmark, leaving a 1 ½-inch opening on the bottom.

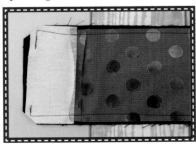

**5** Trim the corners. Flip the bookmark right side out and press.

**6** Top stitch all around the edge.

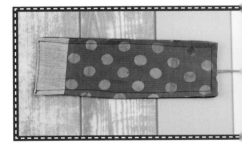

**7** Thread beads onto the cords, and knot in place.

# Beanbag

Critter comforts are important, but you should relax, too! A beanbag chair is the perfect room accessory, and it couldn't be easier to whip together.

## Materials

· 6 yards of fabric
· beanbag filling

## Cut

· six 38-inch squares of fabric

**1** Stack two fabric squares, right sides together. Pin and sew down one side.

**2** Repeat step 1 with three more squares. Each piece of fabric should touch a different side of the center square, to make a plus sign shape.

**3** Match all the corners of the plus sign. Pin and sew them together. Your fabric piece will now look like a box.

**4** Place the remaining piece of fabric on top of the box. The right sides of the fabric pieces sould touch. Sew around the cube, leaving an 8-inch opening.

**5** Flip the bean bag right side out. Fill with the beanbag filling.

**6** Sew the opening shut.

# Bunny Plush Keychain

Carry some character with cute keychains! These bunny plushies come with an easy-to-follow template.

## Materials

- ¼ yard of plush fabric for front, back, and ears
- ¼ yard of fabric for inner ears
- 2 colors of embroidery thread, and embroidery needle
- fiber filling
- jewelry pliers
- keychain

## Cut

- two 2 ½-by-7 ½-inch pieces of fabric for back ears (see pattern on page 47)
- two 2 ½-by-7 ½-inch pieces of fabric for inner ears (see pattern)
- two circles for the face (see pattern)
- 2 inches of embroidery thread for loop

**1** Use the pattern on page 47 to trace and cut out ear and face pieces.

**2** Stack an inner and back ear piece with the right side together. Pin and sew around the edges. Leave the bottom edge unsewn.

**3** Flip the ear right side out, and press.

**4** Fold the assembled ear piece in half at the short side, and press. Mark the center point along the crease line. Unfold it and press another half from the previous fold. Pin and baste.

**5** Repeat steps 2–4 with the second ear.

**6** Use chalk to sketch a face onto the face piece. Use embroidery thread to fill in the chalk marks.

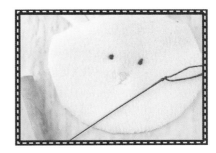

**7** Use chalk to mark where the ears will attach to the face piece. Pin and sew the ears in place.

**8** Wrap some embroidery thread loosely around your finger two or three times. Cut the loose end of the thread.

**Continued on the next page...**

**9** Place the loop between the ears. Pin and stitch into place.

**10** Place the face and back piece with the right sides together. Sew around the fabric. Leave a 2-inch opening along the bottom.

**11** Clip the curved edges. Flip the bunny right-side-out.

**12** Fill in fiberfill through the opening. Then use a slipstitch to close the bunny.

**13** Use pliers to open one of the keychain's jump rings. Slide the ring onto the embroidery thread loop. Then close the ring.

Tip:

Place a piece of thin paper – such as newspaper, tissue paper, or tracing paper – over the template. Then carefully trace the template onto the paper.

Cut the pattern out of the paper. If you're using a more complex pattern, use a highlighter to mark the lines you need to cut.

Set the pattern on top of your fabric. Pin the paper to the fabric, or use weights to hold the paper in place.

Cut out the pattern pieces from the fabric.

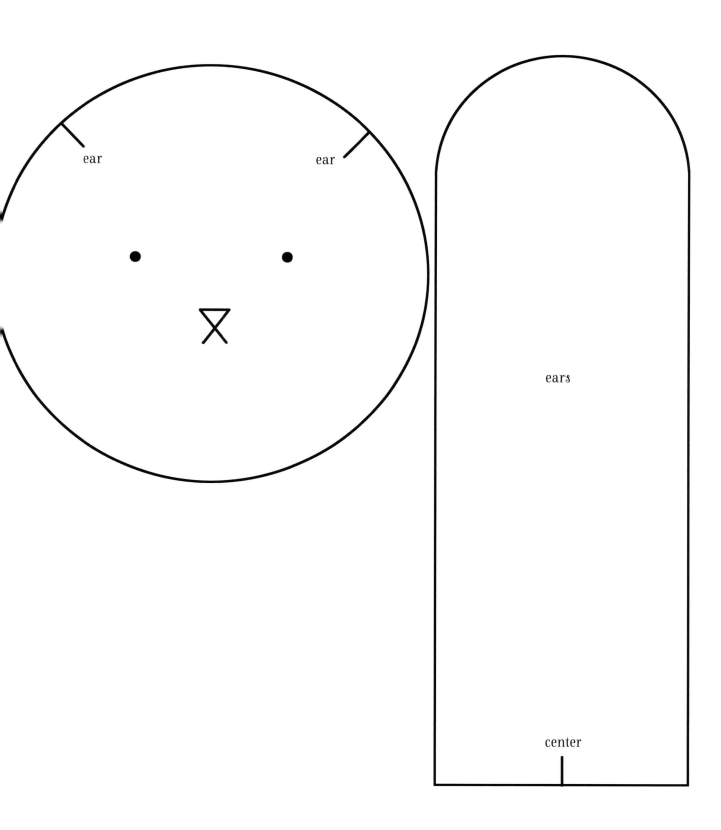

ear

ear

ears

center

47

# Read More

Blum, Nicole. *Stitch Camp.* North Adams, Mass.: Storey Publishing, 2017.

Heynen, Jennifer. *Sew Small: 19 Little Bags: Stash Your Coins, Keys, Earbuds, Jewelry & More.* Lafayette, Calif.: C&T Publishing, Inc., 2017.

Kim, Sue, and Veronica Yang. *Perfect Patchwork Bags: 15 Projects to Sew-From Clutches to Market Bags.* Lafayette, Calif.: Stash Books, an imprint of C&T Publishing, 2016.

# Author Bio

Veronica Yang has worked with her mother Sue Kim with C&T publisher as a featuring designer in the book *Perfect Patchwork Bags.* She also has been operating the website ithinksew.com with her mother for many years. Veronica was introduced to sewing by her mother, who is working in the field of sewing and craft. In her spare time, Veronica enjoys drawing, painting, design, and photography. Veronica lives with her loving parents, two funny yet annoying brothers, along with three cats and two dogs.

# Titles in this Set

Crochet Projects That Will Hook You

Felting Projects You Won't Be Able to Resist

Knitting Projects You'll Purl Over

Seamless Sewing Projects